THE UNIVERSE
OUTER SPACE

IAN RIDPATH

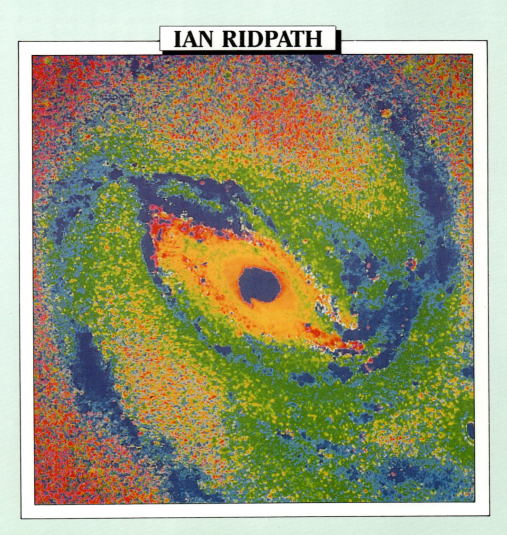

Editorial planning
Philip Steele

MACMILLAN

First published 1987

Published by
MACMILLAN EDUCATION LTD
Houndmills, Basingstoke, Hampshire RG21 2XS
and London
Companies and representatives
throughout the world

Designed and produced by BLA Publishing Limited,
East Grinstead, Sussex, England.

Also in LONDON · HONG KONG · TAIPEI · SINGAPORE · NEW YORK

A Ling Kee Company

Illustrations by Sebastian Quigley/Linden Artists
Colour origination by Chris Willcock Reproductions
Printed in Spain

British Library Cataloguing in Publication Data

Ridpath, Ian
    The universe : outer space. — (Macmillan
    world library).
    1. Outer space — Juvenile literature
    I. Title
    523   QB500.22

ISBN 0-333-44172-9
ISBN 0-333-44179-6 Series

Photographic credits

t = top b = bottom l = left r = right

cover: Science Photo Library

4 Science Photo Library; 6*t* Mansell Collection; 6*b* Ann Ronan Picture Library; 7 Science Photo Library; 12 Michael Holford; 14, 15, 16, 17, 18 Science Photo Library; 19 John Mason; 21*t*, 21*b*, 24, 25, 26, 27, 28, 29, 30 Science Photo Library; 32, 33 John Mason; 34 Science Photo Library; 35*t* Mansell Collection; 35*b*, 36, 37*t*, 37*b*, 40 Science Photo Library; 41*t* Kobal Collection; 41*b* Science Photo Library; 42 ZEFA; 43 Science Photo Library; 44/45 John Mason

Note to the reader
In this book there are some words in the text which are printed in **bold** type. This shows that the word is listed in the glossary on page 46. The glossary gives a brief explanation of words which may be new to you.

Contents

Introduction

Let us suppose we are taking a journey into outer space. We must leave our home **planet** behind. The **Earth** is a great ball of rock which spins around as it travels through space. We are kept on the surface of the planet by a force which pulls everything downwards. The force is called **gravity**. We must travel very quickly in order to break away from the pull of the Earth's gravity.

Only a **rocket** can lift us away from Earth. The rocket shoots up into sky.

When it reaches a speed of over 11 km a second, it can escape the pull of the Earth's gravity. The rocket can keep moving outwards.

The Earth is surrounded by a layer of air, called the **atmosphere**. Out in space there is no air to breathe. We must take air with us in our spacecraft. There is no feeling of 'up' or 'down' in space. We float freely in our spacecraft. We are **weightless**.

Out into space

Let us now steer our spacecraft away from Earth. First, we pass the **Moon**. This small world is our nearest neighbour in space. The Moon is 380 000 km away from the Earth. The Moon travels around the Earth, and the Earth travels around the

◄ An American called Bruce McCandless leaves his spacecraft behind for a view of the planet Earth, far below him. The gravity of Earth cannot pull him downwards. He is floating in space. He carries air and drinking water with him, as there is none in space.

Sun. The path through space of one object around another is called an **orbit**.

Other planets are also in orbit around the Sun. Some of them have moons as well. The Sun and its planets are called the **Solar System**. The Sun is a **star**. It is a great ball of glowing **gas**. We steer our spacecraft away from the Sun, and the inner planets Mercury and Venus.

On our journey, first we pass the planet Mars. Then we come to Jupiter, the biggest planet in the Solar System. Next is Saturn, a planet with bright rings around it. We are now far from the Sun. At last we reach the distant worlds of Uranus, Neptune and Pluto. This is the edge of the Solar System. We are moving into outer space.

Finding out

In this book we shall find out about outer space and what it contains. We shall look at distant parts of the **Universe**. The Universe is everything that exists. It includes all the stars and the space between them. The Earth and the Solar System are only very small parts of the Universe.

▼ This spacecraft is called Pioneer 10. It has already explored the planets of our Solar System. Now it is leaving them far behind and heading for outer space. We have found out all kinds of things about outer space in recent years, but it still holds many mysteries.

The discovery of space

▼ This old picture shows how people once thought of outer space. Until about 500 years ago many people thought that the stars were fixed to a glass shell which curved above the Earth.

Thousands of years ago, people thought that the Earth was the most important thing in the Universe. They thought that the sky must be a hollow shell with the Earth at its centre. The stars in the night sky were small lights fixed to the shell. Every day, the shell turned once around the Earth. At that time, no one knew that it was the Earth itself which was spinning around each day.

As well as the fixed stars, other lights could be seen. They moved slowly among the stars from night to night. These were the planets. Two thousand years ago, people in Greece tried to work out why these lights were moving. They thought that each planet was fixed to a glass shell which moved round in front of the stars.

The Earth in space

In the year 1543, a Polish monk called Nicolaus Copernicus put forward a new idea. He said that the Sun, not the Earth, was at the centre of the Universe. He said that the Earth went around the Sun, like the other planets.

In 1610, an Italian called Galileo Galilei made his own **telescope**. This made distant objects look nearer. He could now see that the planets were other worlds in space. They travel around the Sun and reflect its light. Galileo showed that Copernicus was right.

In 1672, an Italian who lived in France, Giovanni Cassini, worked out that the Sun is about 150 million km from Earth. People began to realize that space was much vaster than they had thought.

Farther and farther

As people built bigger and bigger telescopes, they could see farther and farther into space. They discovered that all the stars in the sky are glowing balls of gas like the Sun, but much farther away from us. The stars in the sky are members of a big group of stars called the **Galaxy**. There are many other galaxies full of stars dotted throughout the Universe.

In 1969, people landed on the Moon for the first time. We have sent machines called **space probes** to look at the planets. We have begun to explore the Solar System. Beyond, lies outer space. What secrets does it hold? At the moment, we cannot send space probes to the stars. They are too far away. We must look at outer space through telescopes.

▶ Compare this picture with the one at the top of page 6. People's dreams of finding out about outer space have come true. Today, telescopes are protected by a curved roof, or dome. They point out at the sky.

◀ Giovanni Cassini lived in Paris over 300 years ago. He was one of the first people to realize how big the Solar System really is. Today we know that space is vast.

How big is space?

Distances in space are vast. The planet Pluto, on the edge of the Solar System, is 5900 million km from the Sun. Rays of light travel through space at 300 000 km per second. Nothing in the Universe can travel faster.

A ray of light from the Sun takes over eight minutes to reach us. Light takes over 4.3 years to reach us from Alpha Centauri, which is the nearest star to the Sun.

We say that Alpha Centauri is 4.3 **light years** away. A light year is the distance travelled by light in one year. It is equal to 9.5 million million km. Distances in outer space are often measured in light years.

The **Space Shuttle** is a spacecraft that can orbit the Earth and then land like an aircraft. If we could travel to the Sun at the top speed of the Space Shuttle, the trip would take over seven months. To reach Alpha Centuri at the same speed would take 160 000 years!

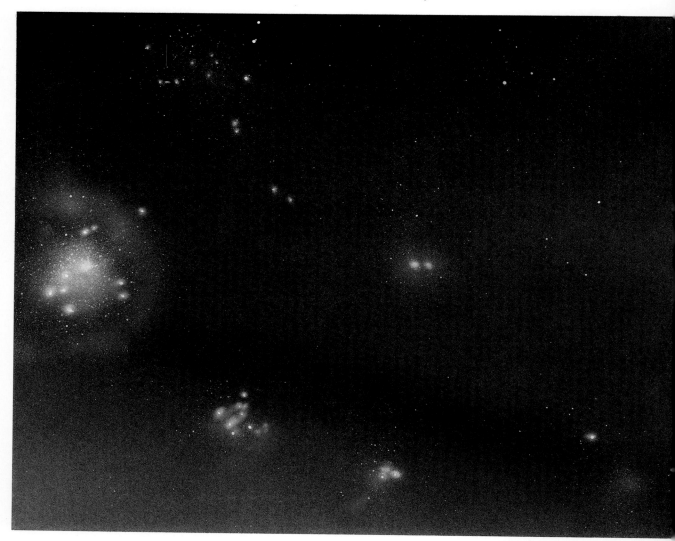

Beyond the nearest star

Our Sun is just one of the stars in our Galaxy. There are about 100 000 million others. The Sun lies at about 30 000 light years from the centre of the Galaxy. Other galaxies are scattered throughout the Universe. The farthest ones we have seen through telescopes lie over 10 000 million light years away. Countless other galaxies lie beyond.

The rays of light we receive from these distant galaxies started their journey shortly after the beginning of the Universe itself.

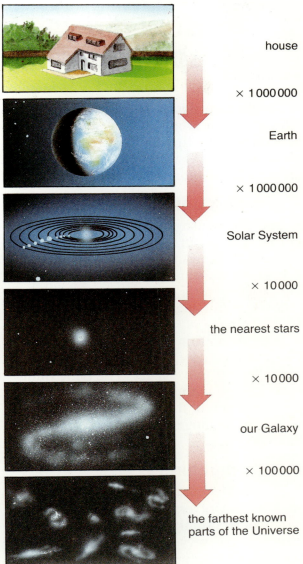

house

× 1 000 000

Earth

× 1 000 000

Solar System

× 10 000

the nearest stars

× 10 000

our Galaxy

× 100 000

the farthest known parts of the Universe

▲ How big is the Universe compared to your home? You can compare the sizes of different parts of the Universe by looking at this chart. For instance, the distance to the nearest stars is about 10 000 times the distance across the Solar System.

◄ It is hard for us to understand distances in outer space. The part of space shown here is about 50 million light years across. The arrow points to our own Galaxy, which is sometimes called the Milky Way. Our Solar System is just a tiny speck within this Galaxy.

How did space begin?

People have always wondered where the Universe came from and how it began. Scientists try to find answers to these questions. People who study the Universe are called **astronomers**.

A growing Universe

In 1929, an astronomer called Edwin Hubble found out something very important. He found that the distant galaxies of stars are moving away from each other. The reason is that the space between them is getting bigger. The whole Universe is stretching.

Imagine dots on the surface of a balloon. As the balloon is filled with air, it swells up. The dots move apart. The same thing is happening with the Universe. It is getting larger all the time, like a balloon. The galaxies move like the dots on the balloon.

In the beginning

The movement of the galaxies is a clue as to how the Universe may have started. Astronomers think that long ago the Universe was very small. It was all squeezed into a tiny ball. For some reason that ball exploded. There was a **big bang**. Space is still flying apart after that big bang.

The speed at which the galaxies are moving outwards tells how long ago the big bang may have happened. It may have taken place between 10 000 million and 20 000 million years ago. On page 35 you can read what astronomers think may happen to the Universe in the future. They still have a great deal to learn about outer space.

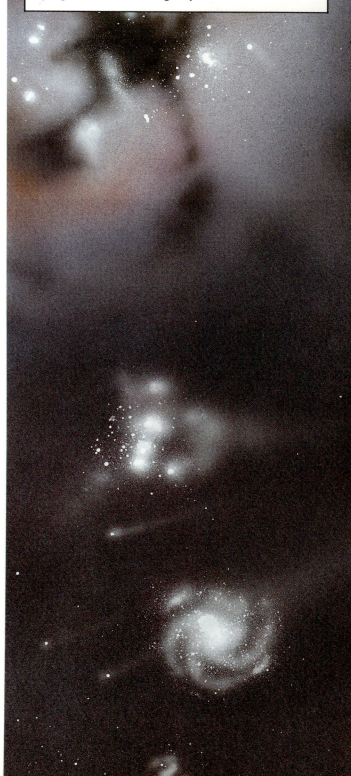

The Universe may have started with a big bang. That would explain why the galaxies are still flying outwards through space.

On the move

▼ This moving model of the Solar System was made in the 1700s. It is called an orrery. It shows how people used to explain the movements they observed in the night sky. The Earth is shown as the most important planet.

Everything in the Universe is moving. The Earth spins once every day. The speed at the **Equator**, the line around the middle of the planet, is 1600 km per hour. We do not notice this movement, because everything else in the world is moving as we do. We do not fly off into space as the Earth spins, because we are held down by the force of gravity.

The spinning Earth travels once around the Sun every year. It orbits at a speed of 100 000 km per hour. The other planets orbit the Sun as well. The inner planets go faster than the outer ones.

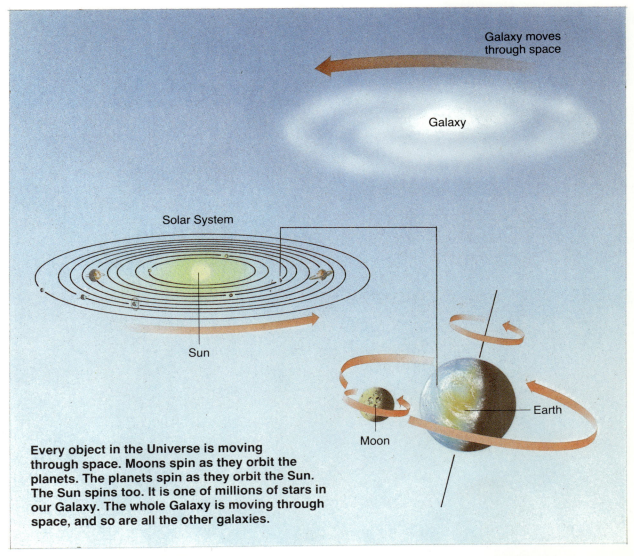

Galaxy moves
through space

Galaxy

Solar System

Sun

Earth

Moon

Every object in the Universe is moving through space. Moons spin as they orbit the planets. The planets spin as they orbit the Sun. The Sun spins too. It is one of millions of stars in our Galaxy. The whole Galaxy is moving through space, and so are all the other galaxies.

Spinning and whirling

The Sun is moving through space, too. It takes the Earth and the other planets with it. They are pulled along by the force of the Sun's gravity. The Sun orbits the centre of our Galaxy at a speed of about 800 000 km per hour. The Galaxy is so big that the Sun takes 220 million years to go around it once. The Sun was born about 4600 million years ago, so it has been around the Galaxy about 21 times. The Galaxy itself is rushing through space as the Universe grows bigger.

All the other stars in the Galaxy are also on the move. They orbit the Galaxy at various speeds. Some stars fall behind the Sun, while others overtake it, like cars on a motorway. The movement of the stars is too small for us to notice with our eyes. The movements show up on photographs which we take through telescopes.

The patterns of stars that we see from Earth are changing very slowly. Hundreds of thousands of years from now, the stars in the night sky will look very different from the way they do now.

What is space made of?

The Universe is mostly made up of empty space, or a **vacuum**. There is a small amount of gas in the space between the planets, stars and galaxies, but it is very much thinner than the air around the planet Earth.

▼ The beautiful Rosette Nebula glows with a pink light. This cloud of gas and dust is amongst the group of stars called Monoceros, the Unicorn.

Gases

Hydrogen gas is the most common substance in the Universe. Stars are made mostly of hydrogen. The stars' gravity holds this gas in a ball shape. In space, though, gas is free to move around. Sometimes it forms clouds called **nebulae**. Most nebulae have no special shape at all.

The Earth's atmosphere is also made of gases. They are not the same as those in a star. **Nitrogen** is one of the most common gases around our planet. Another one is the **oxygen** which we breathe. High above the Earth, the atmosphere thins out. The vacuum of space starts about 100 km above your head.

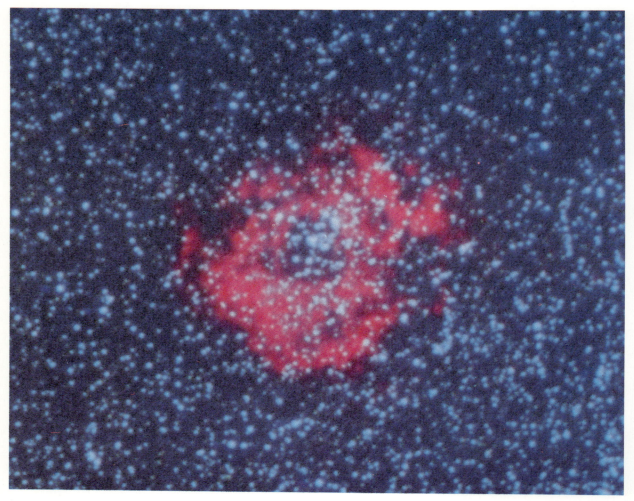

► The Helix Nebula is a round shell of gas which has been given out into space by a dying star. At its centre lies the small centre of the dying star, shrinking and cooling down.

Tiny specks in space

As well as gas, space also contains some tiny specks of **dust**. Dust is found in nebulae, along with gases. We think that stars and planets are born from clouds of gas and dust in space. Stars and some planets grow from the gases. The dust sticks together to build up solid planets, like Earth.

Large nebulae of gas and dust lie between the stars of our Galaxy. Some nebulae are many light years across. New stars are being born all the time from nebulae in space. Other nebulae are formed when some stars die. The dying star puffs off a cloud of gas.

The way things are made

Everything that exists is made of tiny parts called **atoms**. They are too small to see. There are many types of atoms. Hydrogen has the simplest ones. Each has a centre, called a **proton**. A tiny particle called an **electron** shoots around it. Other types of atom have more protons and electrons. Each kind of atom behaves in its own way. That is what makes one substance different from another. The gases in space are different from the dust because they have different kinds of atom. Sometimes the protons and electrons break apart. They move through space on their own.

Rays in space

▲ The Effelsberg radio telescope is in West Germany. It is the largest of its kind in the world. Its dish can be pointed towards objects in space that give out radio waves. The dish picks up the waves. They are passed on to instruments in the nearby building. Here the waves are made stronger and are recorded.

Everything in space gives out rays of **energy**. These rays travel with a wavy motion. They all pass through space at the same speed as light, 300 000 km per second. Light is the kind of ray we know best, because we can see it with our eyes. Light is only one part of the whole family of rays. We cannot see the other types of ray, but we can build instruments to detect them. We can measure the distance between the top of one wave and the next. This is called the **wavelength**.

Light is made up of rays with different wavelengths. We see them as different colours. Violet has the shortest wavelength, about 0.0004 mm. Red light is the longest, with a wavelength of about 0.0007 mm.

Rays we cannot see

Longer waves than red light are called **infra-red**. We cannot see these rays, but we can feel them as heat. Most infra-red rays which come from space are blocked by the Earth's atmosphere.

The longest waves of all are known as **radio waves**. They can have wavelengths of hundreds of metres or even more. Many objects in space give out radio waves. We can pick them up on Earth with **radio telescopes**.

Waves shorter than violet light are called **ultraviolet**. Some ultraviolet rays from the Sun pass through the Earth's atmosphere. They can give us a suntan. **X-rays** are shorter than ultraviolet rays. **Gamma rays** have the shortest wavelengths of all. They are a hundred million times shorter than one millimetre! X-rays and gamma rays are given out by very hot gases in space. They do not pass through the Earth's atmosphere.

Astronomers can study X-rays and gamma rays by sending **satellites** into space. These are machines which orbit the Earth. They can carry instruments which detect rays coming from space.

Other kinds of rays

Cosmic rays are not like the other kinds of rays. They are made up of tiny parts of atoms. They are scattered through space at just under the speed of light. Cosmic rays are thought to be thrown out into space when stars explode.

▼ This picture was made up from signals sent back to Earth by a satellite. It shows X-rays given off by hot gases. The gases surround a galaxy called Cygnus-A, which is 740 million light years from Earth. The green lines are graphs. They show where the most X-rays are coming from.

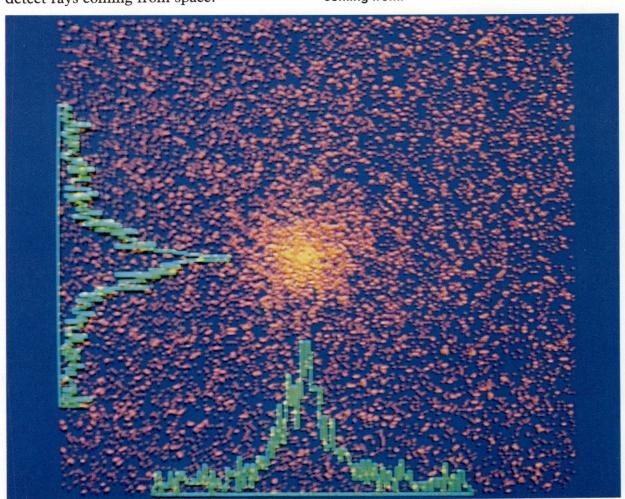

What are stars?

Look at the stars scattered across the night sky. They seem to form patterns. These patterns are called **constellations**. Thousands of years ago, people thought that they could see the shapes of animals and human beings amongst the stars.

The constellations were given names in the Latin language, such as Taurus which means the Bull, Leo, the Lion, and Gemini, the Twins. We still use many of the old names today to describe the parts of the sky where those patterns appear.

Balls of gas

The stars in the night sky look like sparkling points of light. In fact, they are huge glowing balls made of very hot gases.

Betelgeuse

Bellatrix

Mintaka

Alnitak

Alnilam

Saiph

Rigel

Orion the Hunter

▲ The constellation of Orion is easy to spot in the night sky. The stars look as if they are near each other. In fact, they are at different distances from us. Rigel, for instance, is 700 light years nearer to Earth than Alnilam.

◄ When we look at the centre of our Galaxy, the Milky Way, we see a band of stars across the sky. The centre of the Galaxy lies 30 000 light years away. There are countless stars in between.

If we could get close to a star, we would see that it looked a lot like our Sun.

Some stars appear very bright in the night sky. Others are much fainter. There are two reasons for this. One is that some stars really do give out more light than others. The other reason is that stars are all at different distances from us. The closer a star is to us, the brighter it looks. Our Sun would look like a tiny point of light if we could see it from a planet going around another star.

Our Sun is a normal star. All stars give out light and heat like the Sun. They do so because they make energy at their centres. The centre of a star is very hot. The centre of the Sun is about 15 million °C. There, atoms of hydrogen are turned into the atoms of a gas called **helium**. This process gives off energy.

All stars give off energy in the same way. They use up a vast amount of fuel. Six hundred million tonnes of hydrogen is turned into helium inside the Sun every second. The Sun has been using hydrogen at this rate for 4600 million years. The Sun is so big that it has enough gas to keep shining for another 5000 million years.

Other worlds in space

It is likely that planets have formed around many other stars, just as they have formed around the Sun. These distant planets have not yet been seen. They are too far away. One day, we might have proof that there are other planets in outer space. One day we might even travel to them and find worlds like our own.

▼ The M16 Nebula lies in the constellation of Serpens, the Snake. New stars and planets are being formed in this swirling cloud of gases. The stars light up the gases around them.

Star sizes and groups

There are many types of stars and all of them are different sizes. Small stars are called **dwarfs**. They appear faint in the sky. Large stars are called **giants**. The biggest of all are called **supergiants**. They are the brightest stars.

Red dwarfs are stars about one-tenth the size of the Sun. Their red colour means that their surface is much cooler than that of our Sun. **White dwarfs** are about 100 times smaller than the Sun. They are the remains of stars like the Sun that have burned out.

Giants and supergiants are 100 times bigger than the Sun, or even more. Stars like the Sun become **red giants** when they grow old. Stars which are much heavier than the Sun become supergiants when they grow old.

A star's life

Let us follow the life story of an average star. The story starts when a cloud of gas and dust in space shrinks down into a ball. The ball gets hotter at the centre as it gets smaller. In the end, it gets hot enough for hydrogen to turn into helium at its centre. The star begins to shine.

After thousands of millions of years, the star uses up all the hydrogen at its centre. It starts to use the hydrogen in the layers around its centre instead. This gives out more energy. The star swells up into a red giant, and its death is near. The outer layers of gas start to drift off into space. The centre of the star is left behind as a tiny white dwarf.

The biggest stars do not die so quietly. In the end, they blow up in a great flash of light. Stars which explode are called **supernovae**.

▼ The Sun is an average-sized star. Astronomers call it a yellow dwarf. White dwarfs are very much smaller. They are tiny when compared with a huge red giant.

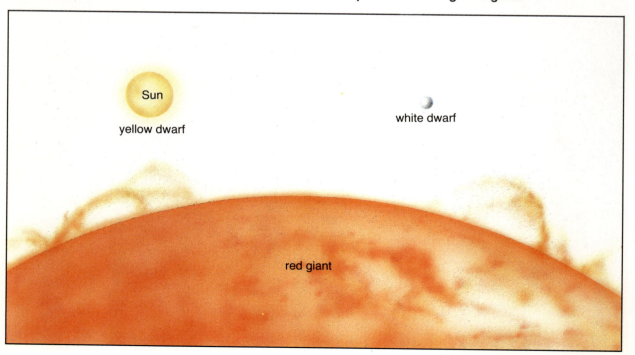

Sun
yellow dwarf

white dwarf

red giant

Star groups

When we look at stars through a telescope we can see that many of them are really double or triple stars. They are held together by gravity. They slowly orbit each other.

In some places we can see large numbers of stars held together in a bunch by the force of gravity. These **star clusters** can contain dozens or hundreds of stars. They have all formed together from the same cloud of gas.

► The star cluster M13 can be seen in the constellation of Hercules. It is 22 500 light years away from Earth.

▼ A small flash of light appears just to the right of the galaxy in the centre of this picture. It is a supernova exploding. It is nearly as bright as the galaxy itself, but after a few months, it will fade away.

Galaxy shapes

Galaxies contain many millions of stars. Some galaxies are huge. They form various shapes. The nearest large galaxy lies two million light years away from us. It can be seen in the constellation of Andromeda. It has a spiral shape. **Spiral galaxies** are very common. Our own Galaxy is a spiral. The Andromeda galaxy looks like our Galaxy, but it is larger. It contains twice as many stars.

Spiral galaxies have curling arms made of stars and gas. There are usually two arms. The arms curve outwards from the galaxy's centre. Some spiral galaxies have a straight bar of stars and gas across their centres. These are called **barred spirals**.

spiral galaxy

spiral galaxy

barred
spiral
galaxy

Rounded shapes

Other types of galaxies are shaped like lemons. These are called **elliptical galaxies**. They have no arms. No one knows why some galaxies have arms while others have not. Giant elliptical galaxies have about ten times as many stars as our own Galaxy. They are the largest galaxies of all. Such huge galaxies are very rare. Some elliptical galaxies are very small. Dwarf ellipticals contain less than one-hundredth the number of stars we have in our Galaxy. Most elliptical galaxies have bright centres with thousands of star clusters.

Shapeless galaxies

Some galaxies have no real shape at all. These are the **irregular galaxies**. They are usually small. We think that there are at least 100 000 million galaxies, of all these types, in the whole Universe.

elliptical
galaxy
(rounded)

elliptical
galaxy
(flattened)

irregular galaxy

Our Galaxy and beyond

▼ A map of our Galaxy shows it as a spiral. Our Sun is a star on the Orion spur. The Orion spur lies between the Perseus arm on the far right and the Sagittarius arm on the right of the spiral.

▼ A map of our Galaxy shows it as a spiral. Our Sun is a star on the Orion spur. The Orion spur lies between the Perseus arm on the far right and the Sagittarius arm on the right of the spiral.

At night we can see a pale band of light across the sky. It is made up of countless stars, and is called the **Milky Way**. All the stars in the Milky Way are members of our own Galaxy. Our Galaxy is sometimes called the Milky Way Galaxy. If we could look at the spiral of our Galaxy edge-on, it would look rather like two plates placed face to face. It is 100 000 light years from side to side, but only about 10 000 light years thick. We see the Milky Way where we look through the thickest part of the Galaxy, along the spiral arms and towards the centre.

Astronomers think that there are at least 100 000 million stars in the whole Galaxy.

That is just a guess, for no one has been able to count them all.

Old stars fill the centre of our Galaxy. Two arms full of younger stars curl outwards from the centre. Our Sun lies on a branch, or **spur**, of one of the spiral arms. It is about two-thirds of the way from the centre to the edge of the Galaxy. Clouds of gas and dust lie between the stars in the spiral arms.

Ball-shaped groups of stars are dotted around the Galaxy. These **globular clusters** contain old stars, like those at the centre of the Galaxy. Their stars were among the first to form when our Galaxy was born, 13 000 million years ago.

Next-door neighbours

The Milky Way's two closest neighbours are the Magellanic Clouds. The Large Magellanic Cloud is about 150 000 light years away. The Small Magellanic Cloud is about 190 000 light years away. Both Clouds are much smaller than our own Galaxy. The Magellanic Clouds are named after Ferdinand Magellan. He was a Portuguese explorer who was the first person to describe them, in 1521. They look like hazy clouds in the southern half of the sky.

▶ The Tarantula Nebula lies in the Large Magellanic Cloud, which is the nearest galaxy to our own. The Cloud is in orbit around our Galaxy. It contains about 10 000 million stars.

▼ A view through our Galaxy shows it as a disc. The thick centre flattens out towards the arms. From Earth, we see the Galaxy from this angle. We call it the Milky Way.

Mapping the galaxies

If we were to travel outwards from the Solar System, we would first pass the stars in our spiral arm of the Galaxy. Then we would move into the next spiral arm. It is called the Perseus arm, because it lies in the direction of the constellation Perseus. The Perseus arm is about 6500 light years from the Sun.

As we travelled onwards, the stars would begin to thin out. We would be coming to the edge of our Galaxy. We would pass a few star clusters and then steer into deeper space. To the south would lie the Magellanic Clouds. To the north would lie the Andromeda galaxy, a vast spiral containing millions of stars.

▼ On a map of the galaxies the larger Magellanic cloud appears next to our own Galaxy. The nearest big galaxy to our own is over ten times farther away. It is called Andromeda.

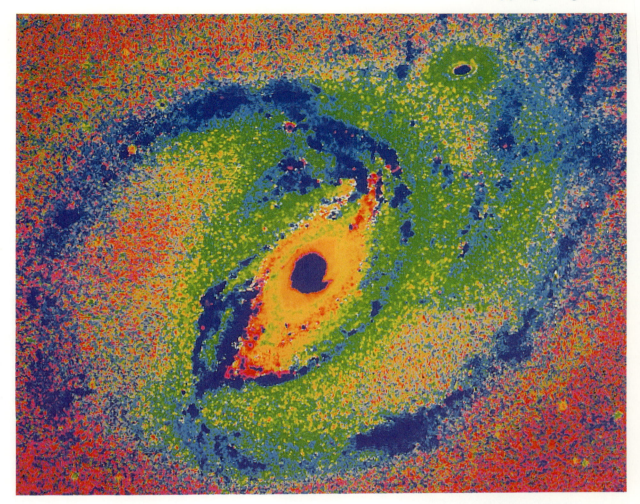

Galaxy groups

The Andromeda galaxy and our own are the largest members of a group of about 40 galaxies. They form the Local Group. Most of these galaxies are small and faint. They do not move apart as the Universe grows, because they are held together by gravity.

The Andromeda galaxy and our own lie on opposite sides of the Local Group. They are two million light years apart. Beyond lie much larger groups of galaxies. One large group lies 50 million light years away. It can be seen in the constellation Virgo. There, over 2500 galaxies form a **galaxy cluster**. Most galaxies seem to lie in clusters.

▲ This computer picture maps out different parts of a galaxy in different colours. Whenever a galaxy is discovered, astronomers give it a number. This spiral is called NGC 1097.

Clusters of clusters

We can see far into space by using big telescopes. We can see clusters of galaxies stretching into the distance. They seem to be bunched together into groups of clusters. These are sometimes called **superclusters**. The Local Group is near the edge of a supercluster. The Virgo cluster lies at the centre of the same supercluster.

Changing galaxies

Galaxies provide us with many puzzles. How did they first form? Some people think that galaxies were born when very large clouds of gas broke up. They then formed clusters and superclusters. Other people think that galaxies were built up from smaller pockets of stars and gas that joined together. Either way, galaxies formed early on in the life of the Universe, over 10 000 million years ago.

Why do galaxies have different shapes? One clue is that spirals spin more quickly than elliptical galaxies. Also, spirals contain a lot of gas. New stars are still forming from this gas. Elliptical galaxies have almost no gas to spare. Stars no longer form inside them. Astronomers used to think that spiral galaxies might turn into ellipticals as they got older. They now think that this is not the case. Both kinds of galaxy seem to be about the same age.

▼ The spiral arm of the Whirlpool Galaxy has been bent. It has been pulled out of shape by a small passing galaxy called NGC 5195.

▲ The galaxy M82 looks as if it is exploding. In fact, it is a spiral galaxy which has run into a cloud of gas and dust in space.

Colliding galaxies

Galaxies can sometimes pass close to each other as they move through space. When this happens, their gravities pull each other into strange shapes.

Sometimes a small galaxy passes a larger one and pulls out one of its spiral arms. This happened to the Whirlpool galaxy.

The small galaxy seems to lie at the end of one of the Whirlpool's arms. In fact it lies behind it.

Another pair of galaxies which have run into each other form the Antennae. This galaxy gets its name because of two long wisps of stars and gas that stretch out into space. They look like the feelers or the 'antennae' on the head of an insect.

If two galaxies pass close enough to each other, one galaxy can swallow up the other one. When this happens it is called **galactic cannibalism**, because the galaxies are eating each other, like cannibals. Many giant elliptical galaxies are thought to be the result of two galaxies that have been joined up in this way.

29

What does space hide?

Outer space is dark. We can see things in space only because of the light that is given out by stars. Some parts of space are hidden from us. In our Galaxy, clouds of gas and dust block off light coming from objects behind them.

In places, the Milky Way looks as if it has holes in it. These holes are not real. They are caused by dark nebulae in front of the stars. One dark nebula lies in the constellation of Crux, the Southern Cross. It is called the Coalsack, because it is so black. It is over 50 light years from side to side. We can see clouds like the Coalsack only because they show up against the lighter areas behind them.

Black holes

The most puzzling objects in space are **black holes**. A black hole is the grave of a dead star. It is formed when a star which is much heavier than the Sun explodes as a supernova. This squashes the centre of the star so tightly that its gravity becomes very strong. This force pulls back light from the star, so that no one can see it any more. The star is now black, so that is seems like a hole in space.

Gravity sucks things into a black hole. Gas and other stars are swallowed up. If a spacecraft passed too close to a black hole, it would be pulled in too. The spacecraft would never be able to get out again, or even signal for help. As things fall into the black hole, the hole gets bigger. Very big black holes may lie at the centre of galaxies. As gas falls towards a black hole, it heats up to many millions of degrees. The hot gas gives out rays of energy.

◀ The Eta Carinae Nebula can be seen from the southern parts of Earth. It is a vast nebula of glowing gases. If you look carefully you can see dark lines across the centre. Dark clouds of dust hide many parts of space from us.

▶ The area of space around a black hole may look like this. It is ringed by very hot gases. The gases and stars around are sucked into the black centre.

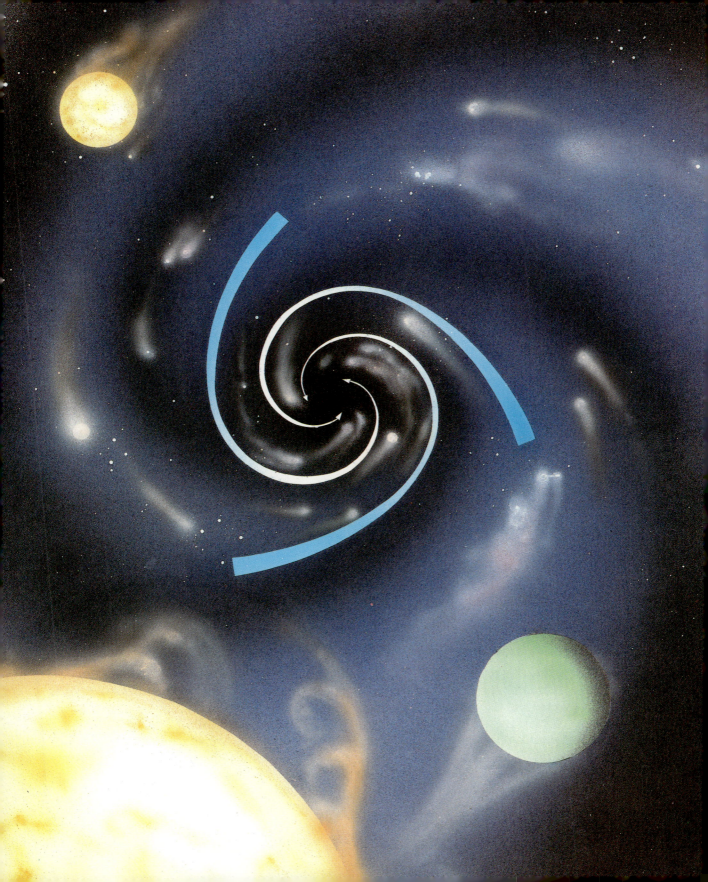

Space puzzles

▼ The nearest radio galaxy to us is called Centaurus-A. It is 16 million light years away. It gives out radio waves a thousand times more strongly than a normal galaxy like Andromeda.

Something is hidden at the centre of our Galaxy. Astronomers cannot see clearly what it is, because there are so many stars and so much dust in the way. Hot gas seems to be streaming around the centre of the Galaxy at high speed. There must be a very heavy object at the centre. It may be a black hole, containing the gas of hundreds of stars.

Some other galaxies show signs of even more going on at their centres. One type is called a **Seyfert galaxy**. This was spotted by an astronomer called Carl Seyfert. Seyfert galaxies are spirals whose centres are very bright. These bright centres are thought to be caused by super-hot gases whirling around a black hole that has swallowed millions of stars.

Other sorts of galaxy give out strong radio waves. These are called **radio galaxies**. The radio waves may come from a black hole, or they may be caused when two normal galaxies run into each other.

Distant energy

The oddest objects of all in outer space are called **quasars**. This is short for 'quasi-stellar object', a phrase which simply means 'something that looks like a star'. Quasars lie far off in space among the galaxies. Some galaxies lie far beyond the galaxies we know. They are the most distant objects we can see in the Universe. Some are over 10 000 million light years away. That means that we see them as they appeared over 10 000 million years ago. At that time, the Universe was still young.

Quasars give out hundreds of times as much energy as all the stars in the Milky Way. All this energy comes from a space not much bigger than our Solar System.

How can quasars produce so much energy from such a small area? They may be made up of very hot gas falling towards a monster black hole. This black hole might weigh as much as 1000 million stars. The gas is so hot that it gives out X-rays. These tell us that a black hole is there. Astronomers think that quasars lie at the centre of young galaxies.

The more scientists manage to solve the great puzzles of the Universe, the more questions are raised.

▼ Two quasars can be seen in this X-ray picture of space. The small quasar at the top left of the picture lies 10 000 million light years away. The large one at the bottom right of the picture was the first quasar ever to be found. The dots between them show up X-rays coming from space.

Questions of gravity

▼ The remains of a supernova give out radio waves.This computer picture has been given colours to show up where the waves are coming from. Today, we can use satellites and computers to solve many of the mysteries of outer space.

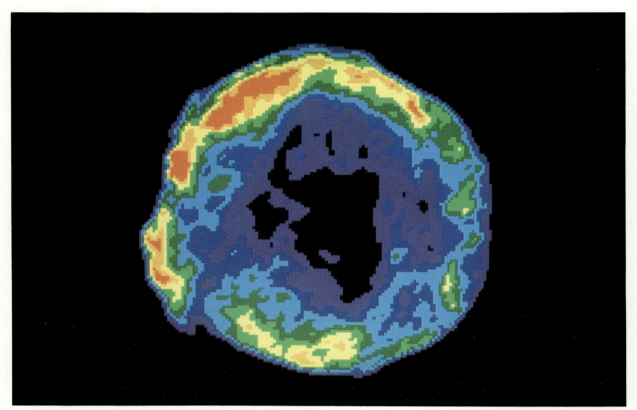

In outer space, things happen that we could not imagine on Earth. Many of these things are to do with gravity. Scientists have not yet found out all there is to know about this pulling force. They are trying to find out more about gravity by looking at how it works in space.

One of the things gravity does is to bend the path of light and other rays. In 1915, a scientist named Albert Einstein worked out that this is what happens. Normally, the wavy rays that pass through space travel on a straight course. Einstein said that light and radio waves are bent slightly when they pass close to the Sun. We now know that this is true. Black holes have an even

greater effect than the Sun. The strong pull of the black holes bends the rays so much that they cannot escape.

Big galaxies have an odd effect on rays which are coming from behind them. Rays from distant quasars are bent around the galaxy. This makes it look as if there are two quasars, one on either side of the galaxy. The light from the quasar has been split in two by the gravity of the galaxy.

Einstein also said that stars which blew up would cause ripples in space. He called these ripples **gravity waves**. These waves are so weak that scientists have not yet been able to find them. They are still searching for them.

Putting on the brake?

What will happen to the Universe in the future? Will it carry on growing? Again, it all depends on gravity in space. If there are enough stars and galaxies in the Universe, the pull of their gravity might slow down the movement of the galaxies.

In the end, the galaxies might stop moving outwards. The galaxies would then start to fall together again. This 'big crunch' might be followed by another big bang, far in the future.

Astronomers have found out that the outward motion of the galaxies has slowed down only slightly since the Universe began. The slowing down does not seem to be enough to stop the Universe moving outwards. Space may carry on getting bigger and bigger for ever.

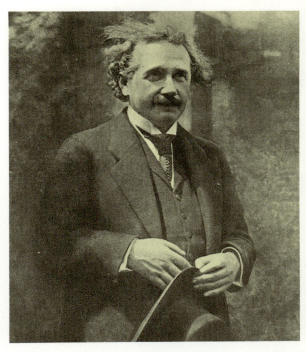

▲ Albert Einstein was born in Germany and later lived in the USA. His ideas changed our understanding of how the Universe works.

▼ Radio telescope dishes search the skies from the deserts of New Mexico, in the United States. Twenty-seven dishes form this Very Large Array.

Finding out more

If we put telescopes on top of high mountains, we can see the sky more clearly. Today, we can put telescopes even higher. We can send them into space, above all the gases that surround our planet. The Earth's atmosphere causes two problems for astronomers. Firstly, it blurs our view of space. It stops us seeing things in detail. Secondly, it stops many rays, such as X-rays and gamma rays, from reaching the ground.

Telescopes and other instruments can be

◀ A Space Shuttle is launched by rockets, but it returns to Earth like an aircraft. The Shuttle can be used to carry satellites into space.

sent into orbit around the Earth. They can be put on satellites. The satellites can travel around the Earth at a height of several hundred kilometres. The satellites pick up rays from space. They use **radio signals** to send the information back to the Earth.

Telescopes for the future

One new telescope is called the Hubble **Space Telescope** (HST). It is named after Edwin Hubble. The HST will be launched by the Space Shuttle and go into orbit around the Earth. The HST uses mirrors to reflect rays of light. The HST is a **reflecting telescope**, like the big ones on Earth. It has a mirror 2.4 m across, and is the biggest telescope ever sent into space.

▼ The Hubble Space Telescope will be carried into space by the Space Shuttle. It will be able to look far into outer space.

▲ The Einstein Observatory being prepared for its launch in 1978. This satellite took the X-ray picture on page 33. New X-ray satellites are being planned.

The HST will be able to look farther out into space than we have ever seen before. It will be able to see objects in outer space 100 times clearer than the best telescopes on Earth can. It will help us to find out about distant objects such as quasars. It may tell us more about how the Universe began and how it works.

Other satellites will be put into space to look at special types of rays. The Infra-Red Space Observatory (ISO) will pick up heat rays from space. It will carry on the work started in 1983 by the first of its kind, the Infra-Red Astronomy Satellite (IRAS). New satellites will also be launched to study X-rays in space. In the far future we may build telescopes at a base on the Moon.

Space travel

Satellites which are sent into orbit around Earth can tell us a lot about space. We have also sent space probes to look at other planets in the Solar System. Space probes do not have people on board. They are machines sent to look at objects in space.

Four of the probes which have been looking at the planets will soon leave the Solar System far behind. They will travel into outer space. Pioneer 10 was the first probe to pass beyond the orbit of the planet Neptune. It did this in June 1983. Three other probes are following it into the Galaxy. They are called Pioneer 11, Voyager 1 and Voyager 2. They will all stop working long before they reach the stars. At the speed they are going, it would take them nearly 100 000 years to reach the nearest star, Alpha Centauri!

Starships

The problem with getting to the stars is that they are so far away. If we want to

send space probes to look at the stars, we must build new types of spacecraft that can go much faster than today's rockets. One way of doing this would be to use **nuclear power**. Nuclear power uses the same kind of energy that makes the Sun give out its rays. The energy is made by joining together the centres of different atoms.

Starships using nuclear power would be built in space. They would be much bigger and heavier than any rockets in use today. They might be able to travel at speeds of 100 million km per hour. They would send back pictures of the star and show if there were any planets around it.

These starships will not be built for a long time yet, and the first ones will not have people on board. It will probably be many hundreds of years before people leave for the stars. When they do go, they may be able to live and work on planets around other stars.

▼ A starship of the future speeds through space. A journey to the stars would take many years. Whole families would live on the starship. People would die during the journey, and babies would be born. When the starship arrived, the people from Earth could make their homes on a distant planet.

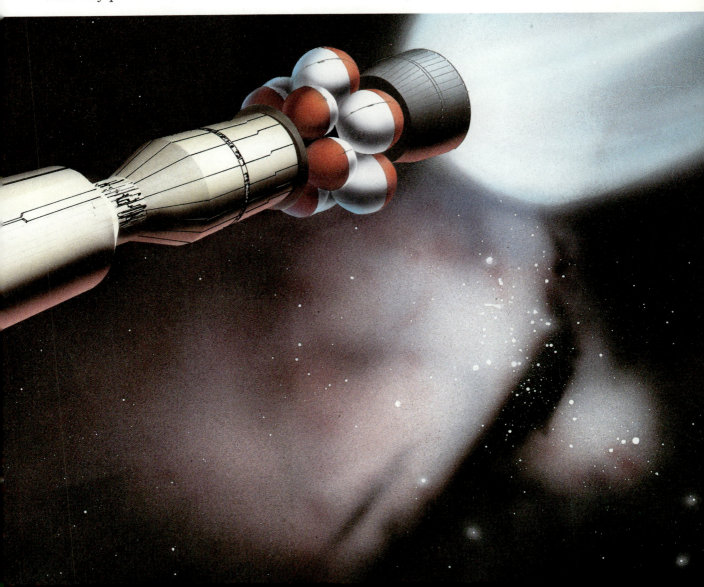

Life in outer space

▼ From space, the Earth appears as a blue and white planet. Two-thirds of its surface is covered in water. The white clouds float in an atmosphere of air. All kinds of living things can survive on the planet.

Our planet Earth is a very special place. It has all the right things needed for life. It has air, water and a mild temperature. If it was closer to the Sun, like the planet Venus, it would be too hot for life. If it was further away, like Mars, it would be too cold. As far as we know, the Earth is the only planet in the Solar System which has life on it.

Living things are made from simple substances such as hydrogen, oxygen and nitrogen. **Carbon** is found in all living things on Earth. All these things are found in the clouds of gas and dust where stars and planets are born.

Astronomers think that one star out of every ten in the Galaxy may have planets around it. That would mean that there are many millions of solar systems like ours in the Galaxy. There may even be many planets like the Earth in outer space. Could there be other planets with life on them?

New worlds

If other life has grown up, it must be on a planet going around the right kind of star. We are lucky that the Sun is a long-lived star. If it had died out quickly, we would not be here. If the Sun had been a faint red dwarf, the Earth would have been too cold for life to start. If the Sun were much brighter, the Earth would be too hot to live on. Not all planets can have life on them.

Even so, it is very likely that there are other forms of life in space. An American astronomer called Carl Sagan has worked out that there could be living beings, able to think, on a million planets in our Galaxy. There would also be many other planets which support life forms such as animals and plants, which cannot think.

▲ This strange-looking creature appeared in the film *Return of the Jedi*. Beings from other planets might look very different from us.

► The stars in the night sky shine down on the Earth's forests. Do any of these distant suns have planets of their own? Are there other worlds in outer space with plants and living creatures?

Space messages

We have all read books or seen films which show how humans of the future will travel between the stars. Stories like this are called **science fiction**. One day science fiction may come true. Could it be that beings from other planets in the Galaxy have already travelled in outer space?

Some people think that the Earth is being visited by spacecraft from other worlds. Strange **unidentified flying objects** (UFOs) are sighted from time to time. Most of these sightings can be explained very simply. They are really bright stars and planets, or shooting stars. Some may be aircraft or satellites. Sometimes the people who see these things do not know what they are. They report them as UFOs.

There is no reason to suppose that we could not explain the sightings if we knew more about them. There is no proof that the Earth has ever been visited by people from other worlds.

Space signals

One way of making contact with other beings in space is to send signals. It is easier than making long journeys. Astronomers have begun to listen for radio messages that might be coming from other worlds. The signals would be very faint, but they could be picked up by large radio telescopes.

▼ Do UFOs really exist? Many people claim to have seen strange objects in the sky. These objects may sometimes be clouds with strange shapes. Some may be balloons or aircraft. Some photographs which have been taken are really fakes.

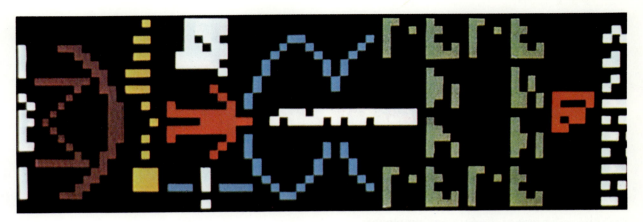

▲ In 1974, a radio message was sent to the stars from Earth. The message will arrive in 22 500 years time. Perhaps there will be beings able to understand the radio message? The signals can be arranged to make a picture. The picture shows the atoms which make up life on Earth, as well as the shape of a human body and other details.

▶ The Voyager space probes being prepared for launch. Each probe carried a record with sounds of animals, human languages and music.

We have sent out messages of our own. Signals have been sent into outer space from radio telescopes on Earth. If they were picked up by a thinking being on another planet, the signals could be arranged into patterns of numbers or pictures. The pictures would tell other beings what we look like.

The Pioneer and Voyager space probes that are leaving the Solar System also carry messages. On the Pioneer probes a picture shows two humans and a diagram of our Solar System. One day we may find a message sent to us from another world. Then we shall know for sure that we are not alone in space.

43

Fact File

The night sky is divided up into 88 star patterns, or constellations. They are of various shapes and sizes.

The oldest stars in our Galaxy are thought to be about 13 000 million years old. They were born at the same time as the Galaxy itself. The Galaxy is over twice the age of the Sun and its planets. The Universe must be older still. It may be four times older than the Sun and the Earth.

The lightest stars weigh about one-tenth as much as the Sun. The heaviest stars we know about are over 100 times the weight of the Sun.

The word 'galaxy' comes from a word in the Greek language, meaning 'milk'. The Milky Way looks like a hazy white band across our sky. That is how our Galaxy got its name. The word 'nebula' comes from a Latin word meaning 'mist'. Clouds of gas in outer space do look rather like wisps of mist or fog.

Out of every 100 atoms in our Galaxy, 92 are hydrogen and 8 are helium. Only one atom in a thousand forms any other substance.

All the hydrogen in the Universe, and most of the helium, was made during the big bang that started the Universe moving outwards. All the other types of atom have been made since then. They have been formed inside stars. That includes all the atoms that make up the Earth, even our own bodies.

How warm is it out in space? The temperature of empty space has been measured at $-270°C$. This very slight warmth in the Universe is energy left over from the big bang.

▶ The North American Nebula lies in the constellation of Cygnus, the Swan. This glowing cloud of gas and dust lies about 3000 light years from our Solar System.

Glossary

astronomer: someone who studies the stars and planets and other objects in space

atmosphere: the layer of gases that surrounds a planet or a star. The Earth's atmosphere is the air that we breathe

atom: the smallest part of a substance that can still behave like the rest of that substance

barred spiral: a kind of galaxy which has a bar of gas and stars running across its centre, and two arms closely circling the outside

big bang: the huge explosion which may have started the Universe moving outwards

black hole: the remains of a star. It has very strong gravity. It sucks in every object around it in space. It even pulls back rays of light. That is why we cannot see a black hole

carbon: a substance found on Earth in fuels, foods and all living things. Carbon is also found in space

constellation: a group of stars as they are seen from Earth

cosmic ray: a tiny piece of matter which streams out through space

dust: tiny pieces of solid matter. A lot of dust floats around in space

dwarf: a very small star. White dwarfs are about 100 times smaller than the Sun. Red dwarfs are about ten times smaller

Earth: our home planet. Earth is one of the nine planets which are known to circle the Sun

electron: the smallest part of an atom

elliptical galaxy: a kind of galaxy which is shaped like an oval. Some are almost round, and some have a flattened shape

energy: the power given out by stars or other objects in space, or by machines

Equator: an imaginary line around the middle of a planet or a star. The Equator is halfway between the two poles

galactic cannibalism: the swallowing up of one huge group of stars by another group

galaxy: a group of millions and millions of stars, all loosely held together by gravity. Our own Galaxy is called the Milky Way

galaxy cluster: a group of galaxies

gamma rays: one of the group of rays which have shortest wavelength. Gamma rays cannot pass through the Earth's atmosphere

gas: a substance that is neither liquid nor solid. Air is made up of several gases

giant: a very large star. Some giants are over 100 times the size of our Sun

globular cluster: a group of very old stars that cling together in the shape of a ball

gravity: the force that pulls objects towards each other. The Sun's gravity keeps the Earth in orbit around it. The Earth's gravity keeps us on the Earth. Gravity makes objects fall and gives them weight

gravity wave: a surge of force that may pass through space when a star explodes

helium: a gas which is the second lightest substance in the Universe

hydrogen: the lightest gas in the Universe. The Sun is made of hydrogen gas

infra-red rays: rays with a wavelength longer than the red waves we can see, but shorter than radio waves. We feel them as heat

irregular galaxy: a galaxy which has no special shape

light year: the distance light travels in one year. It is equal to about 9.5 million million km

Milky Way: a band of hazy gas and stars we can see in the night sky

moon: a smaller body that travels around a planet. Most planets have moons. The planet Jupiter has 16 moons. The Earth has only one Moon

nebula: a cloud of gas and dust in space

nitrogen: a gas found in the atmosphere of some planets. Nitrogen has no colour, smell or taste. It does not burn

nuclear power: the energy created when the centres of certain atoms are forced together

orbit: a path made through space by one thing going around another. The planets move in orbit around the Sun

oxygen: a gas found on Earth in water and air. Oxygen is very important to all plants and animals. We cannot breathe without oxygen

planet: a body in space which moves around a star such as the Sun. The planet shines by reflecting the light of the star. A planet can be made of rock, metal or gas

proton: part of the centre of an atom. Each different kind of atom has a different number of protons in its centre

quasar: an object far away in space which looks like a star. Quasars give out far more light and other rays than galaxies

radio galaxy: a galaxy which gives out powerful radio waves

radio signal: a pulse or sound carried by a radio wave. Messages can be sent from one place to another using radio signals

radio telescope: a telescope made to pick up radio waves instead of light from space. It has a big metal dish

radio wave: a ray which has the longest wavelength of all, from about one millimetre to many kilometres

red dwarf: a star that is one-tenth the size of the Sun. Red dwarfs are much cooler so they do not give out much light

red giant: a dying star that swells to 100 times its normal size

reflecting telescope: a kind of telescope which uses mirrors to collect and focus rays of light

rocket: something which burns fuel to move forwards or upwards very quickly. Rockets are shaped like cylinders and used for fireworks, signals, and launching spacecraft

satellite: a small body in orbit around a larger body in space. The Moon is a satellite of Earth. We also call spacecraft that orbit around the Earth satellites

science fiction: stories told about what may happen in the future

Seyfert galaxy: a type of galaxy which gives out an unusual amount of light from its centre

Solar System: the Sun and all the objects that orbit it, such as planets and moons

space probe: a machine sent from Earth to study objects in space. It does not carry people

Space Shuttle: a special kind of spacecraft which is also able to act like an aeroplane. It takes off upwards like a rocket but after re-entry glides in to land like an aeroplane on a long runway

space telescope: a large telescope that stays in space. It is put into orbit around the Earth. Telescopes on the Earth must look through the gases of the Earth's atmosphere. Space telescopes can get a much clearer view of space

spiral galaxy: a kind of galaxy with a flattened shape, and arms curving out from the centre

spur: a branch off the spiral arm of a galaxy. Our Solar System lies on the Orion spur of the Galaxy

star: a glowing ball of gas that gives off its own light and heat. The Sun is a star

star cluster: a group of stars which are very close together

Sun: the star nearest to the Earth. The Sun gives us all our heat and light

supercluster: a huge group of many galaxies that are close together

supergiant: a very large or bright giant star

supernova: the explosion of a very big star at the end of its life

telescope: an instrument for looking at distant objects, or for picking up rays that come from them

ultraviolet rays: rays which have a shorter wavelength than the violet light we can see

unidentified flying object: an object sighted in the sky which cannot be explained. Some people think that UFOs may be spacecraft from other planets in outer space

Universe: all of space and everything in it

vacuum: an empty space with no air or any other matter in it

wavelength: the distance between the top of one wave and the top of the next. It is how we measure different kinds of rays, such as light, which travels with a wavy motion

weightless: describes the state of floating freely in space

white dwarf: the remains of a dead star, which is very small

X-ray: a ray with a very short wavelength. X-rays are longer than gamma rays but shorter than ultraviolet rays. The rays are given out by very hot gases in space

Index